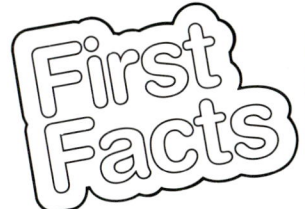

Hospital Work

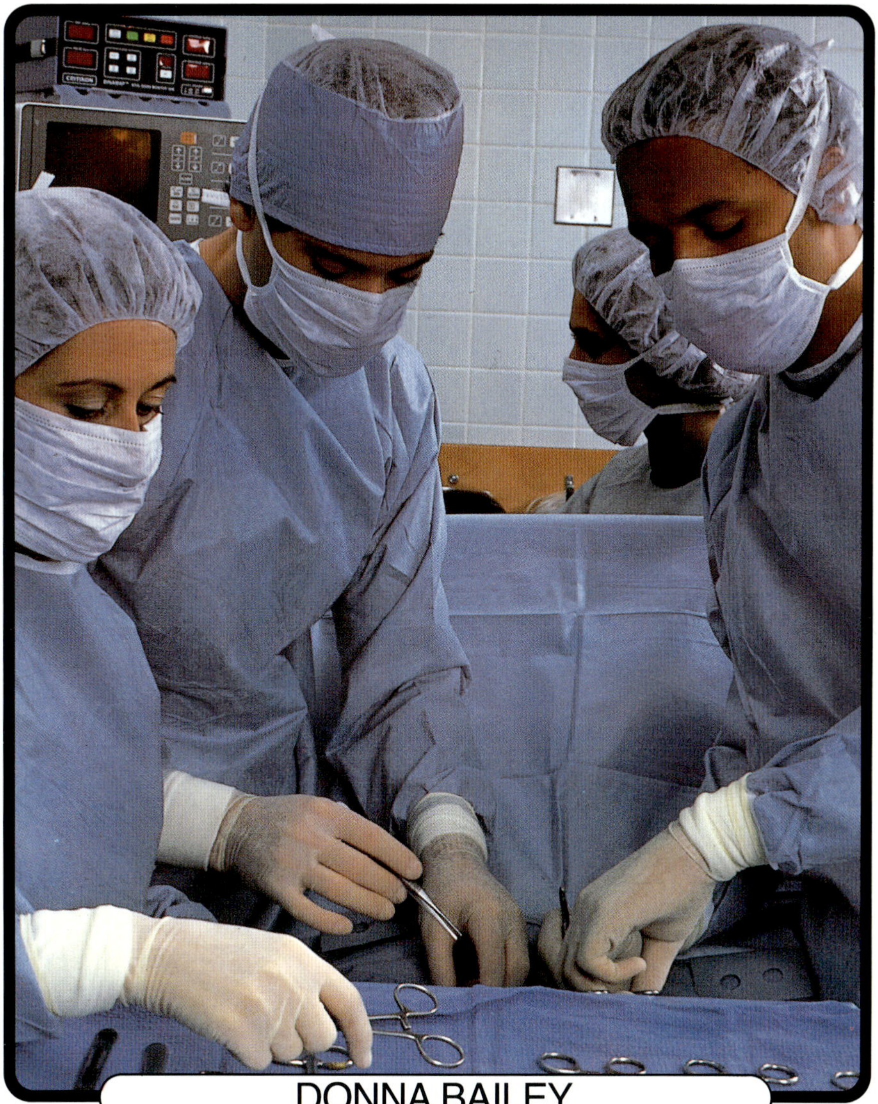

DONNA BAILEY

HEINEMANN

How to use this book

This book tells you lots of things about hospitals. There is a list of Contents on the next page. It shows you what each double page of the book is about. For example, pages 12 and 13 tell you about 'Out-patient clinics'.

On all of these pages you will find some words that are printed in **bold** type. The bold type shows you that these words are in the Glossary on pages 46 and 47. The Glossary explains the meaning of some words which may be new to you.

At the very end of the book there is an Index. The Index tells you where to find certain words in the book. For example, you can use it to look up words like germs, infection, clinic and many other words to do with hospitals

© Heinemann Educational Books Ltd
Artwork © BLA Publishing Ltd

First published in 1991 by Heinemann Children's Reference
A division of Heinemann Educational Books Ltd
Halley Court, Jordan Hill, Oxford OX2 8EJ
Companies and representatives throughout the world

Material used in this book first appeared in *Hospital*.

British Library Cataloguing in Publication Data
Bailey, Donna
Hospital work.
1. Hospitals
I. Title II. Series
362.11

ISBN 0–431–00944–9

Printed in Hong Kong

Contents

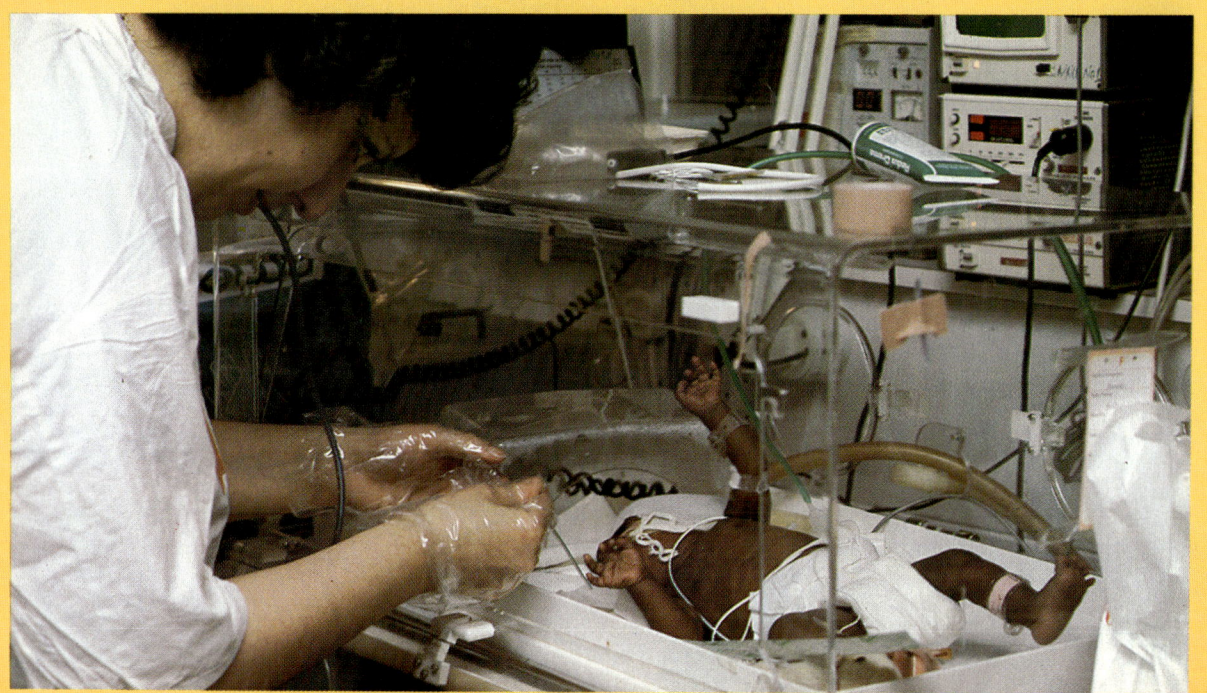

Introduction

A hospital is a place where very sick
people can be cared for until they
are well enough to go home.
Doctors, nurses and the other people
in the hospital care for the patients
during their stay in the hospital.
The staff are ready to give **emergency**
treatment to save a patient's life at
any time of day or night.

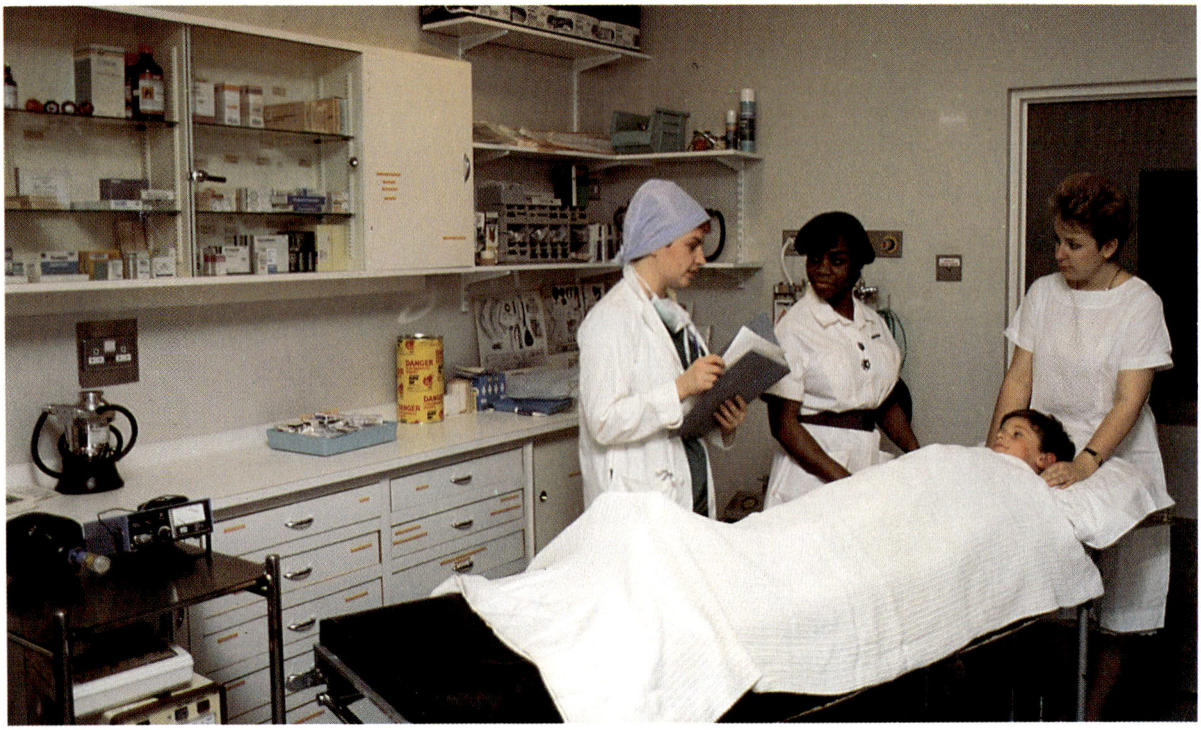

4

Many people are sent to hospital by
their family doctor so that they can
see a **specialist**.
Hospitals work together with family
doctors to look after the health of
the people who live nearby.
For example, many hospitals have
clinics for mothers and babies where
babies' health and weight are checked.

Hospitals in history

The earliest hospitals looked after wounded soldiers after a battle. Later on priests and nuns took care of sick people.

People used herbs to cure their illnesses. In China, doctors and **herbalists** like the one in our picture still make use of herbal medicines today.

This old building in Beaune, France is still used as a hospital.

Early hospitals were dirty and very crowded, and sick people often had to share their beds with others.
Many people died from **infection**.

In the 1800s the French scientist Louis Pasteur discovered that **germs** cause infection and **disease**.
He showed that wounds do not become infected if they are kept clean.

In 1854 Florence Nightingale was the first person to teach nursing.

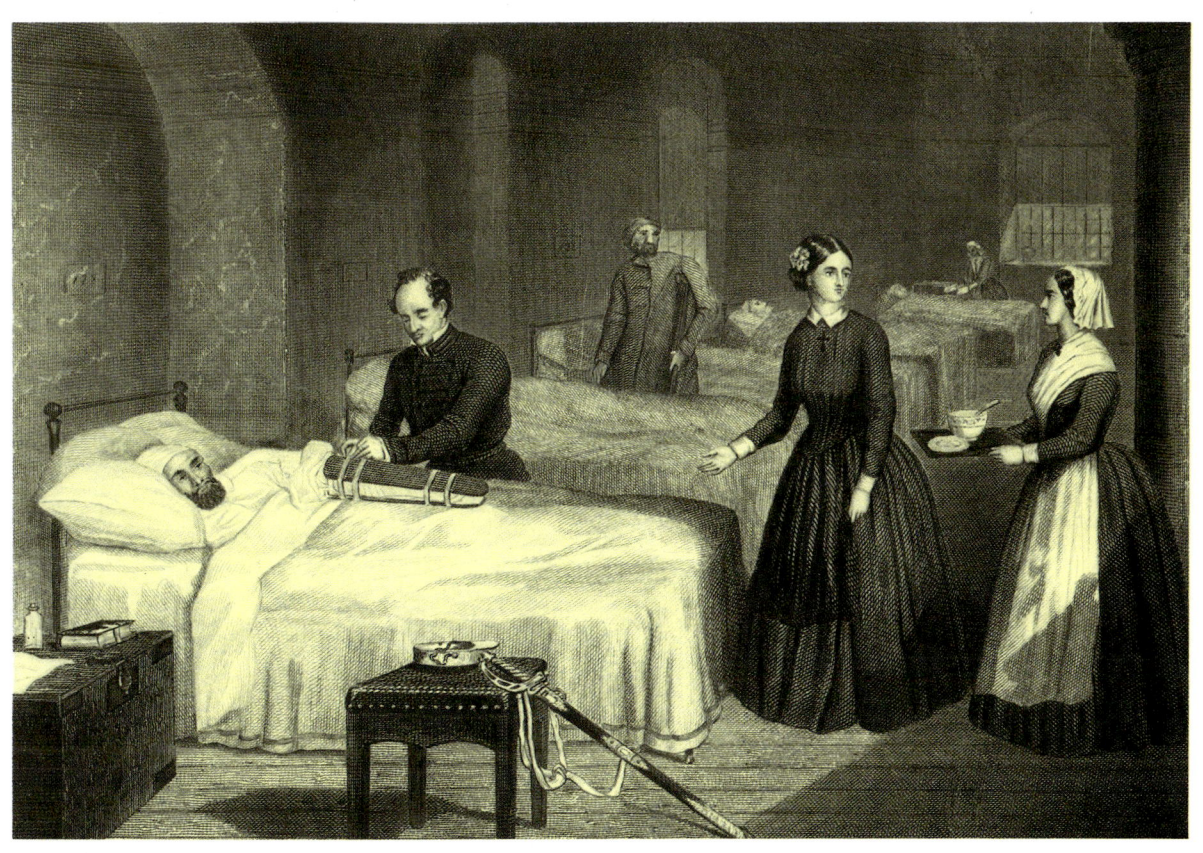

Around the world

Many countries don't have enough
money to build hospitals to care for
sick people who may live in small towns
and faraway villages.
In these countries, **paramedics** like
the one in our picture visit regularly
to check on people's health.

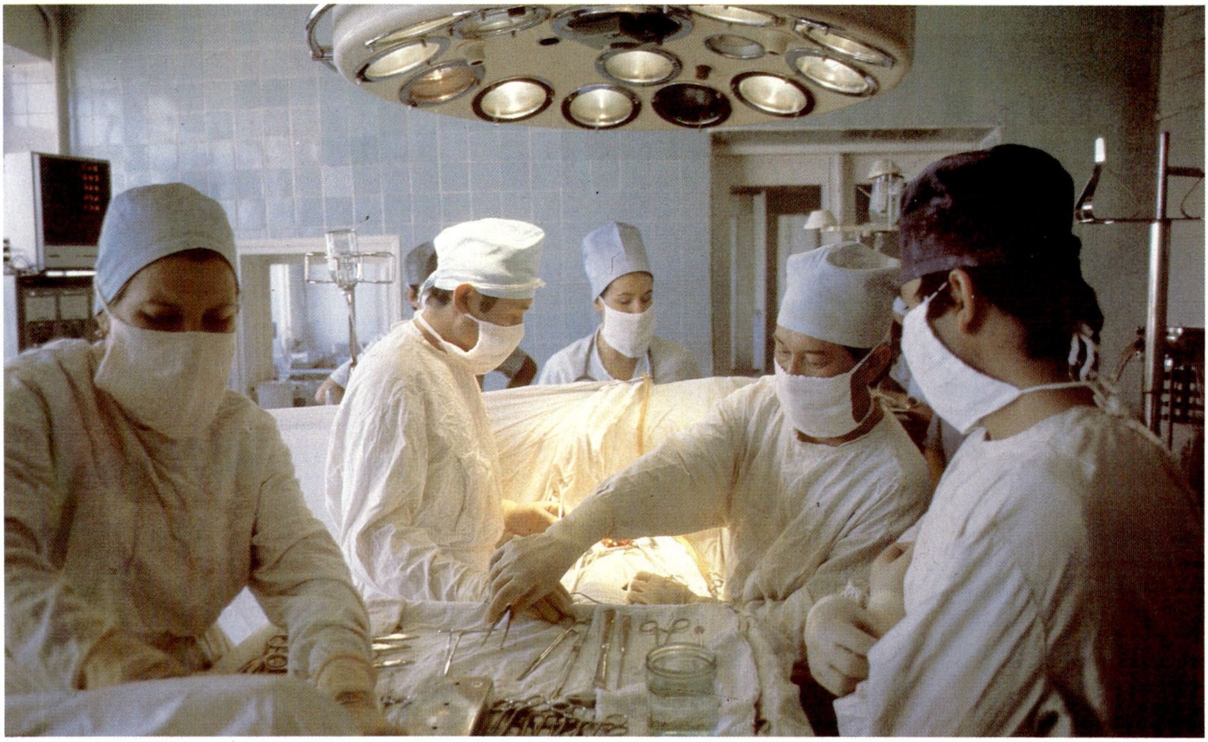

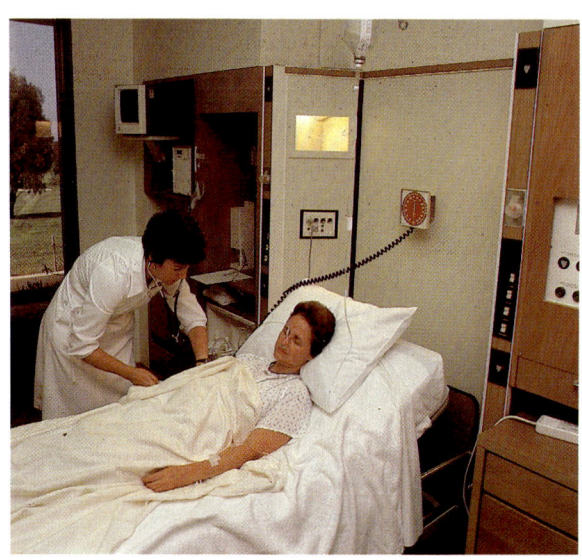

Modern hospitals are very expensive to build. They need a lot of staff and special equipment to look after their patients.

Some hospitals are built by the government. The patients do not pay for their treatment.

In private hospitals, patients must pay for their treatment and for their medicines.

▲ Hospitals in the Soviet Union are free.

▼ A private hospital in the United States

Inside a hospital

Our picture shows the many different departments of a large hospital.

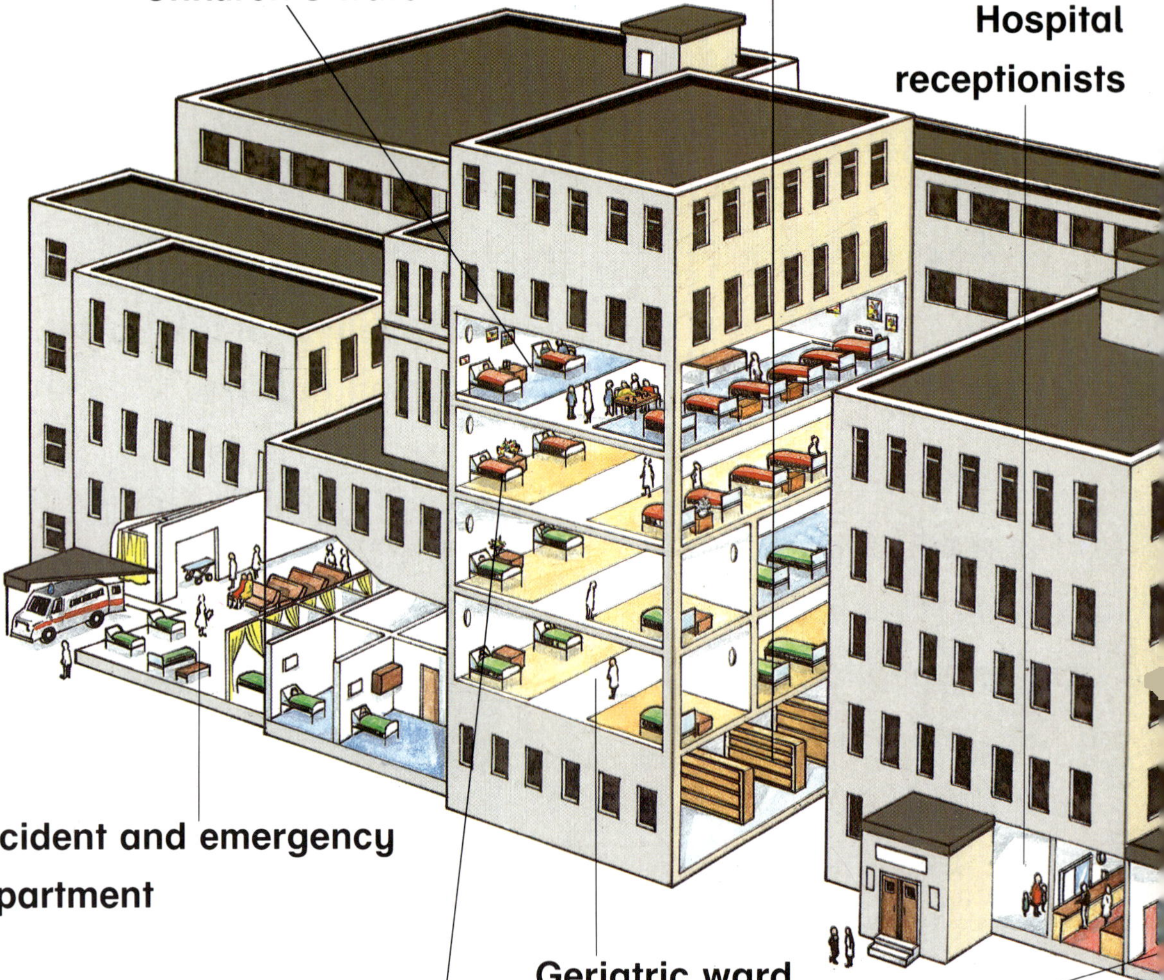

Children's ward

Medical stores

Hospital receptionists

Accident and emergency department

Men's ward

Geriatric ward

Hospital administrator's office

Sick people are cared for in **wards**.
There are separate wards for men and
for women, for children, and for
mothers having babies.

Operating theatre

Hospital laboratory

Kitchens

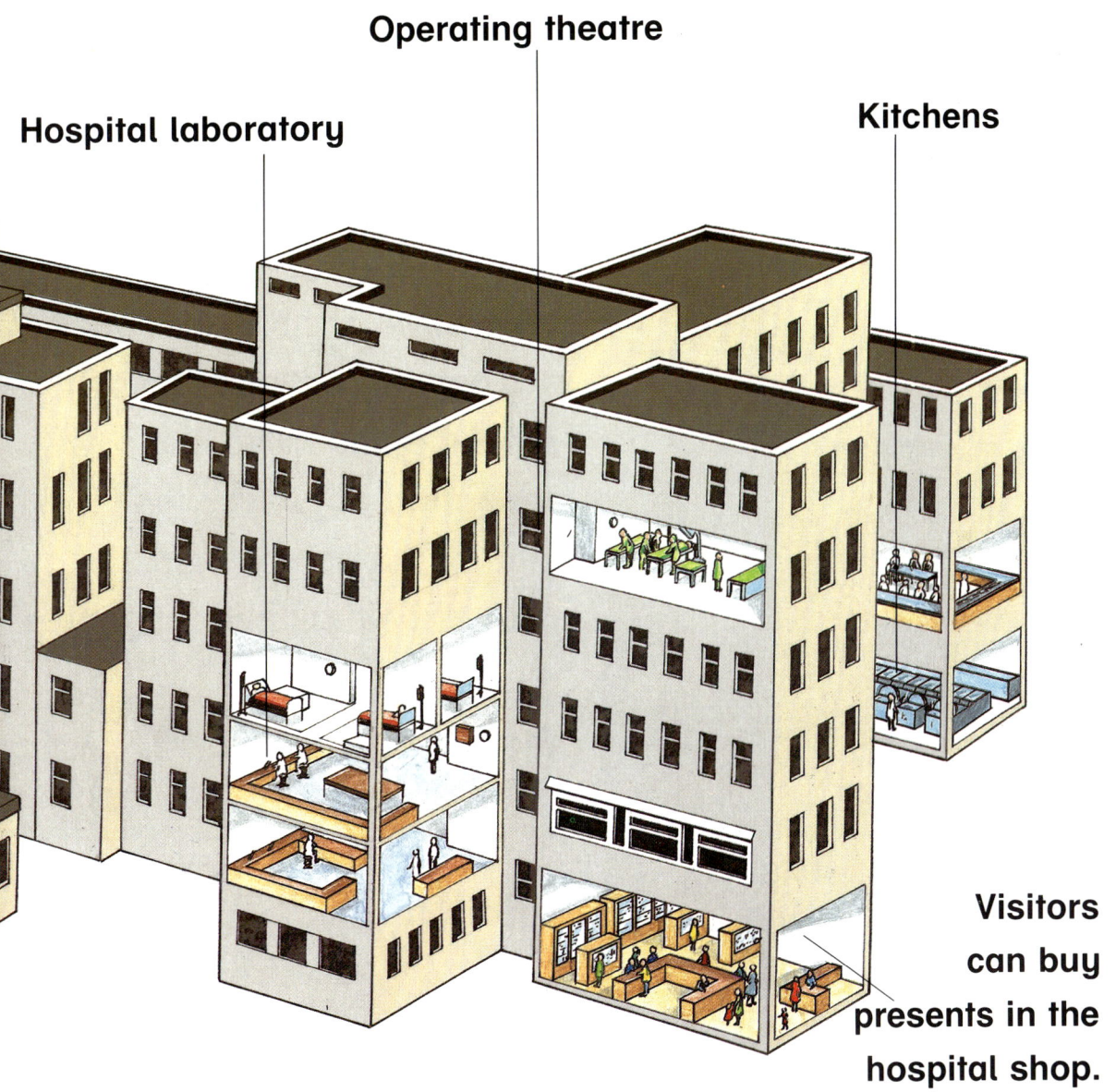

**Visitors
can buy
presents in the
hospital shop.**

Out-patient clinics

Many people visit hospital as **out-patients**.

They may need special medical treatment, or need tests for various diseases. They make an appointment to see a specialist at one of the out-patient clinics.

Each clinic deals with a certain medical problem. One may specialize in eye problems, or illnesses of the blood, another with the ear, nose and throat. Out-patients can also be given **X-rays** to see if they have any broken bones.

When an out-patient arrives at the clinic, the **receptionist** checks the time of the appointment. Nurses help by checking the patient's **blood pressure** or giving any basic tests before the patient goes in to see the specialist.

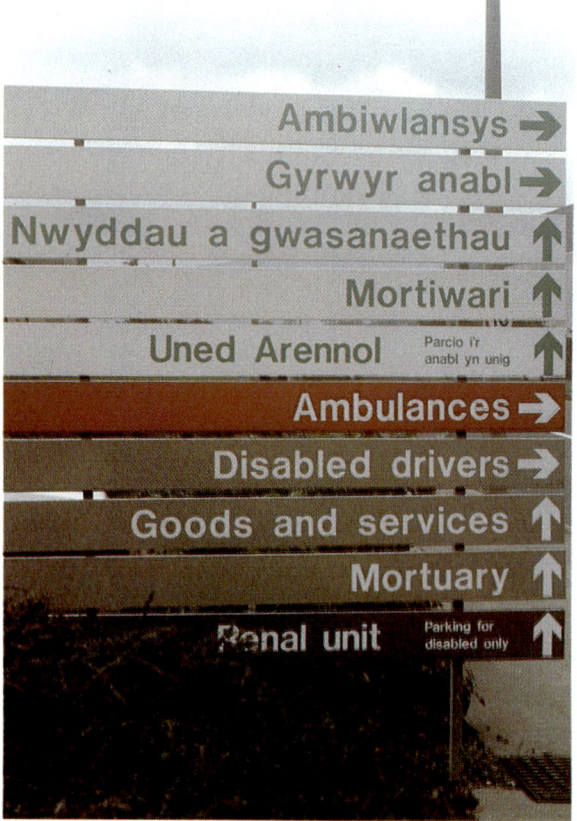

Signs tell the hospital visitor where to go.

Checking an appointment in an out-patients' clinic

▼ Taking a patient's blood pressure

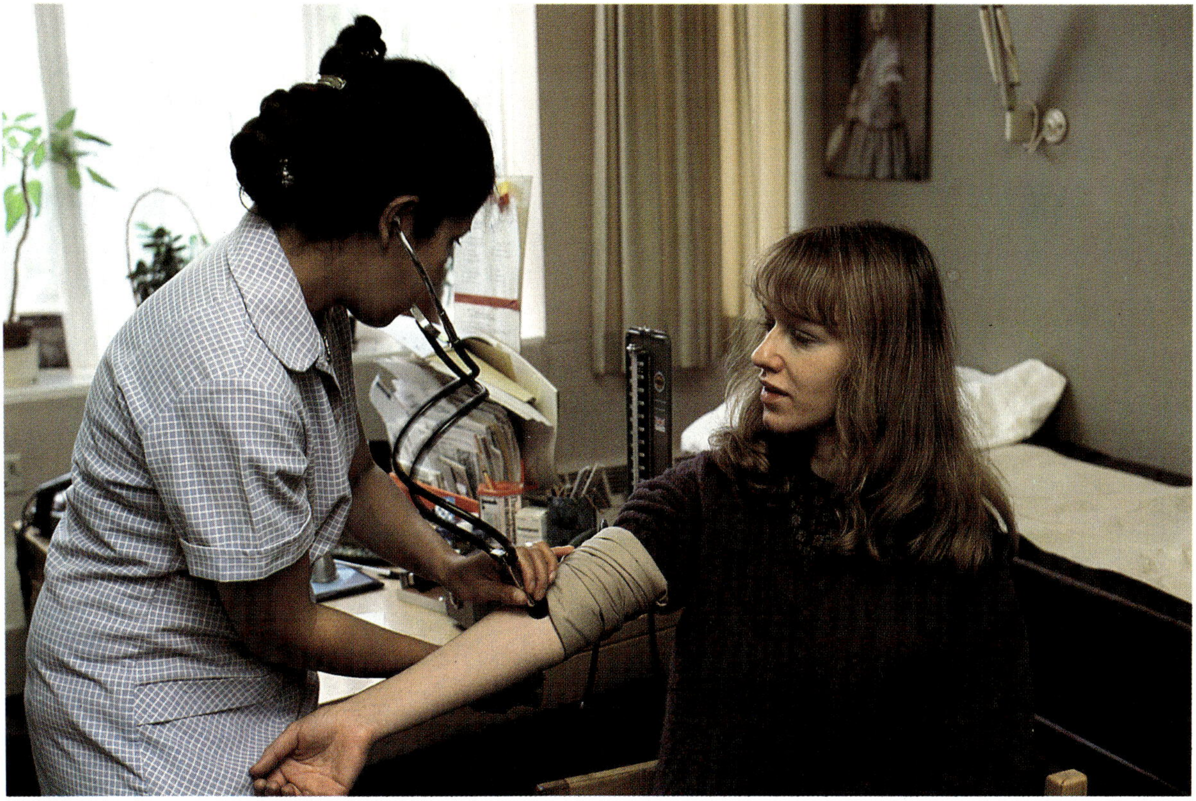

Emergency!

Every year, millions of people are hurt in accidents and need urgent treatment at a hospital.

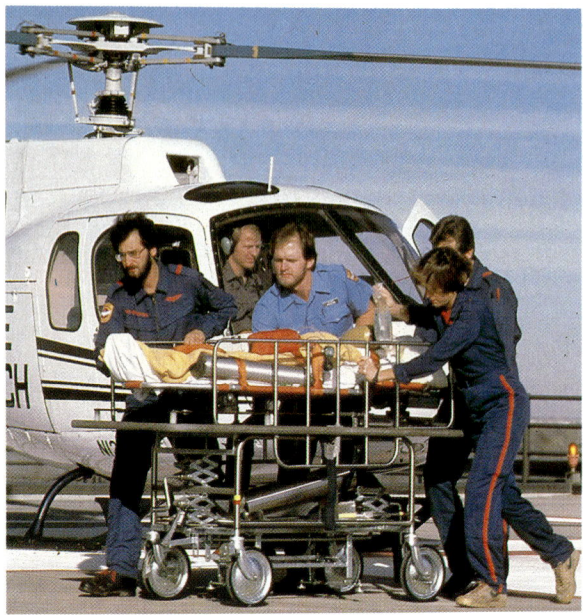

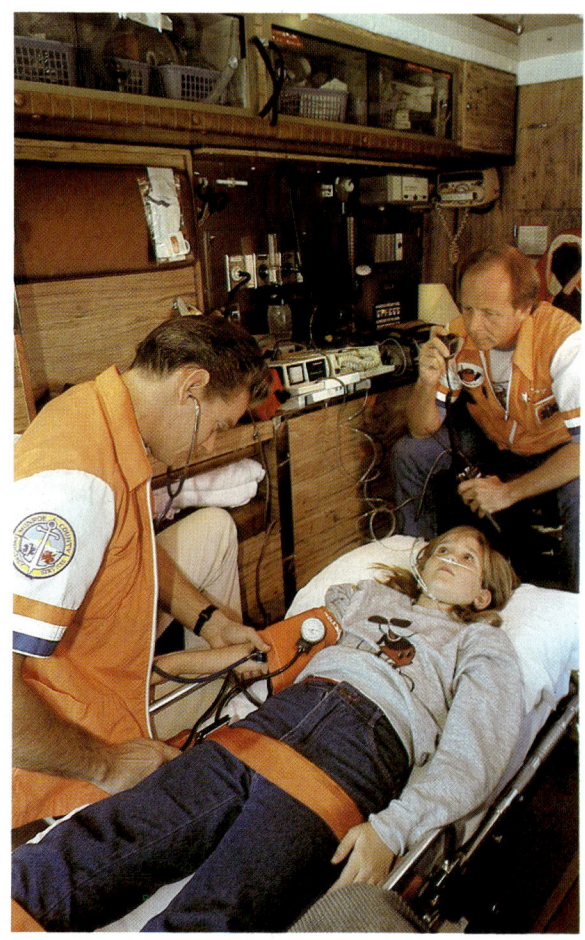

An ambulance crew looking after a young patient

If someone has a serious accident or a sudden illness, you can telephone a special number and ask for an ambulance.
The ambulance crew takes the patient to hospital.
The crew is trained in **first aid** and can give emergency treatment to sick and injured people.

All ambulances have lots of equipment
to help save a patient's life.

In some countries, helicopter
ambulances fly to places far away.
They can get there faster than an
ordinary ambulance.
In Australia and Africa, small
aircraft of the flying doctor
services take patients to hospital.

When an ambulance arrives at the
hospital, the patient is taken to the
accident and emergency department.
The doctors and nurses here are
trained for every kind of emergency.

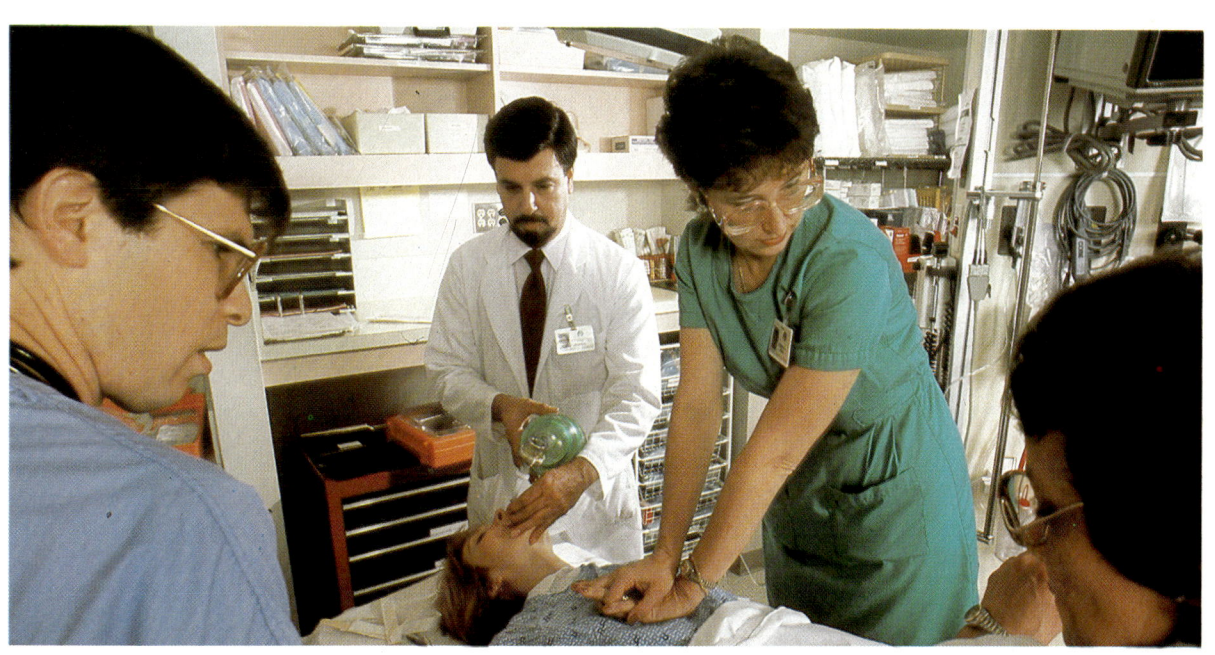

In the wards

The wards of a hospital are usually
large rooms with several beds in them.
The nurses look after the patients in
the wards and give them their medicines.
   A doctor visits each patient in
every ward every morning to check
that the patient is getting better.
Medical students often come with the
doctor to learn how to treat illnesses.

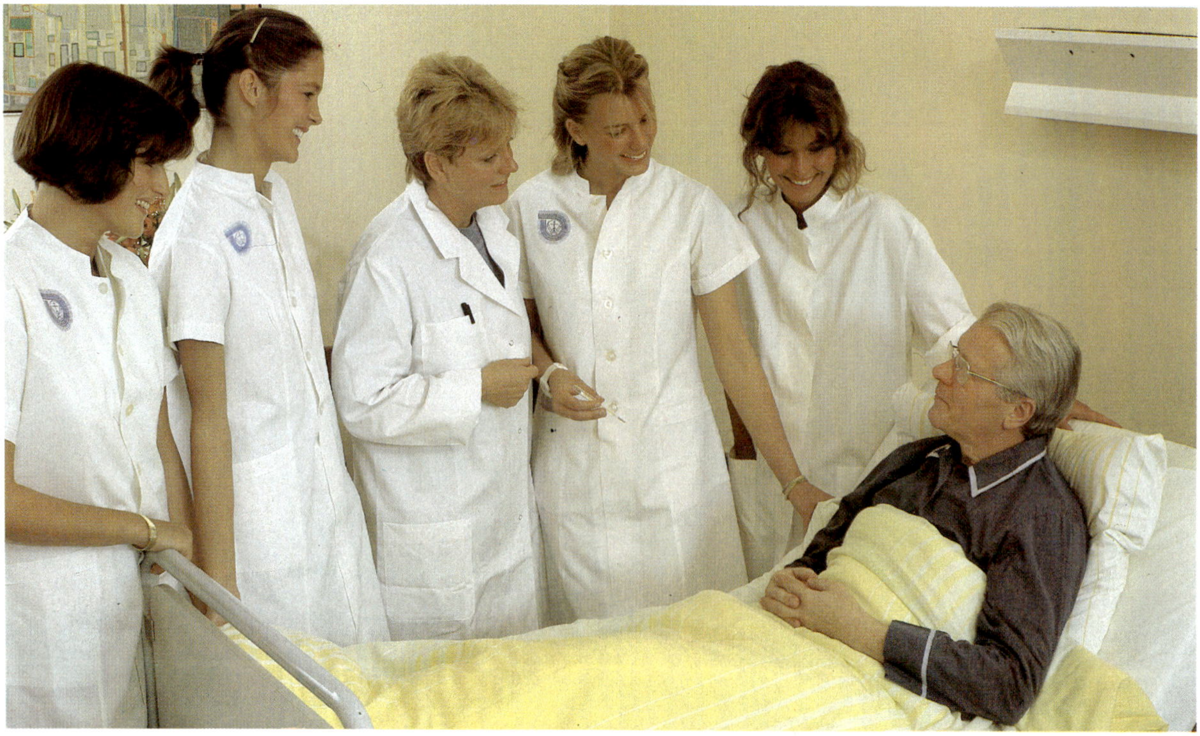

Patients often borrow books to read from the library trolley.

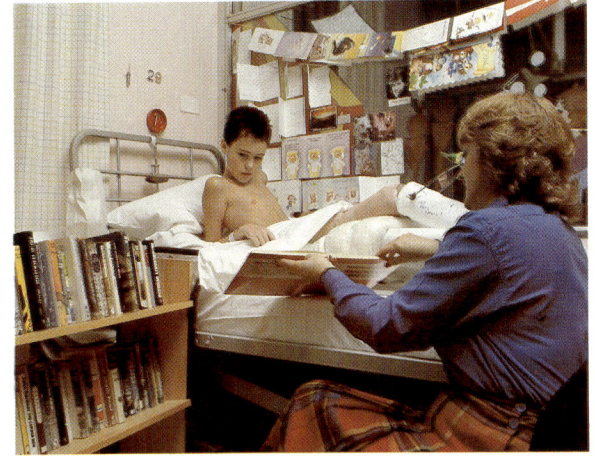

During visiting hours, family and friends may visit the patients.
They often bring them gifts of flowers or fruit.
In some countries visitors have to travel a long way to the hospital.
They may stay in the hospital buildings or camp in the hospital grounds.

Visitors to an African hospital often camp outside the hospital and cook food for the patients.

17

The children's ward

The children's ward is a friendly place, with pictures on the walls and toys and games for the children to play with. Doctors who treat children are called **paediatricians**.

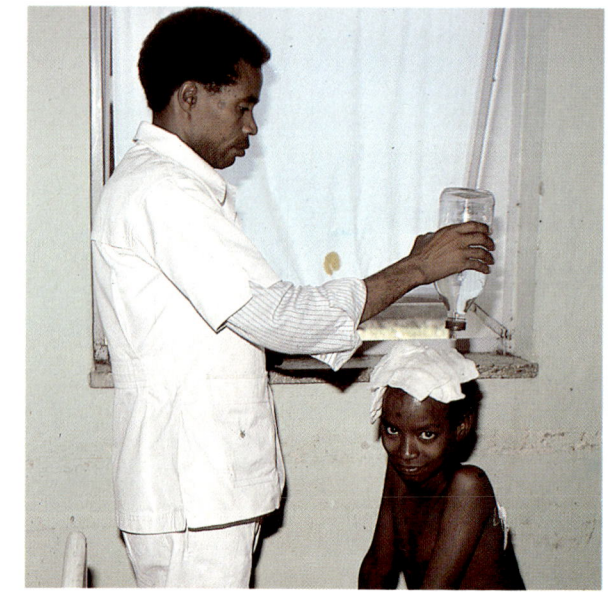

A paediatrician at work

18

Children can usually have visits from
their parents at any time of the day.

Very young children may be worried
and afraid of staying in a hospital.
The nurses are trained to talk to the
children and tell them about their
illness and their treatment.
The nurses comfort worried parents too.

Sometimes the nurses use dolls like
the one in our picture to show a sick
child the parts of the body that may
be causing pain, or which may need an
operation.

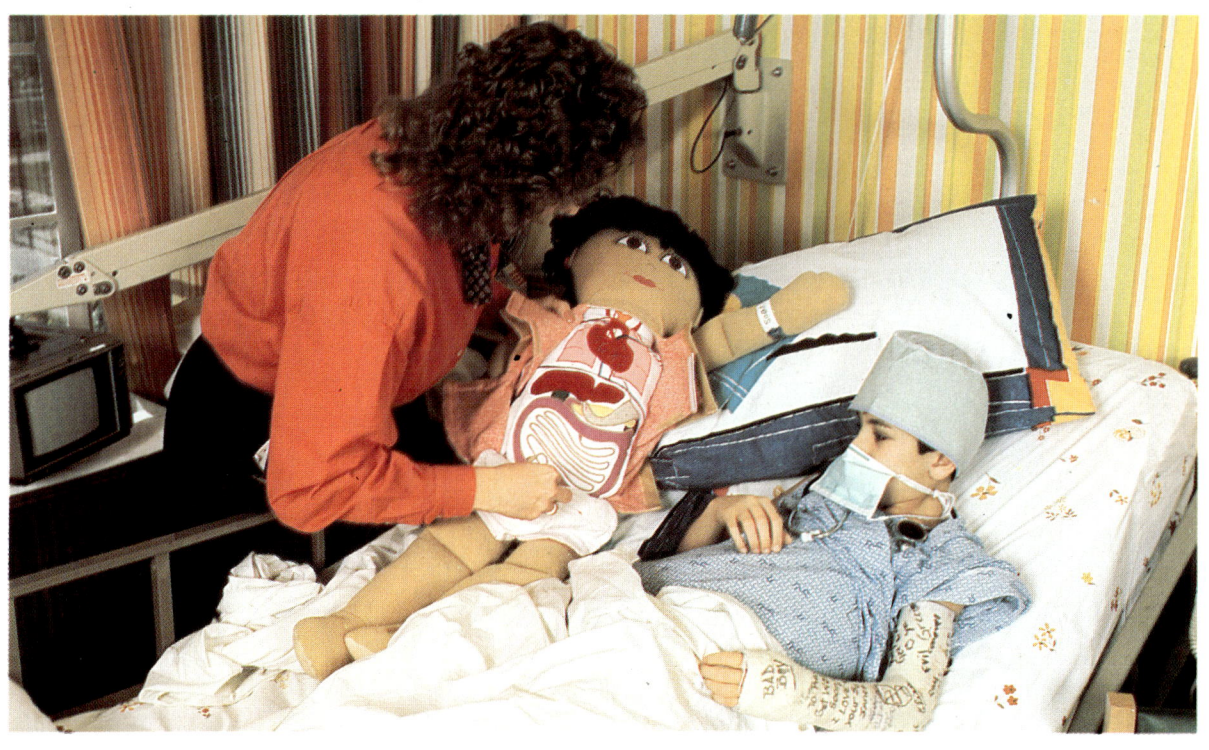

Mothers and babies

Many mothers give birth in hospital.
They go into the labour ward where
they are cared for by **obstetricians**
during the birth of their babies.

After the baby is born, the nurses
wash it and check that it is healthy.
The mother and baby are then taken to
the maternity ward where they stay
until they are ready to go home.

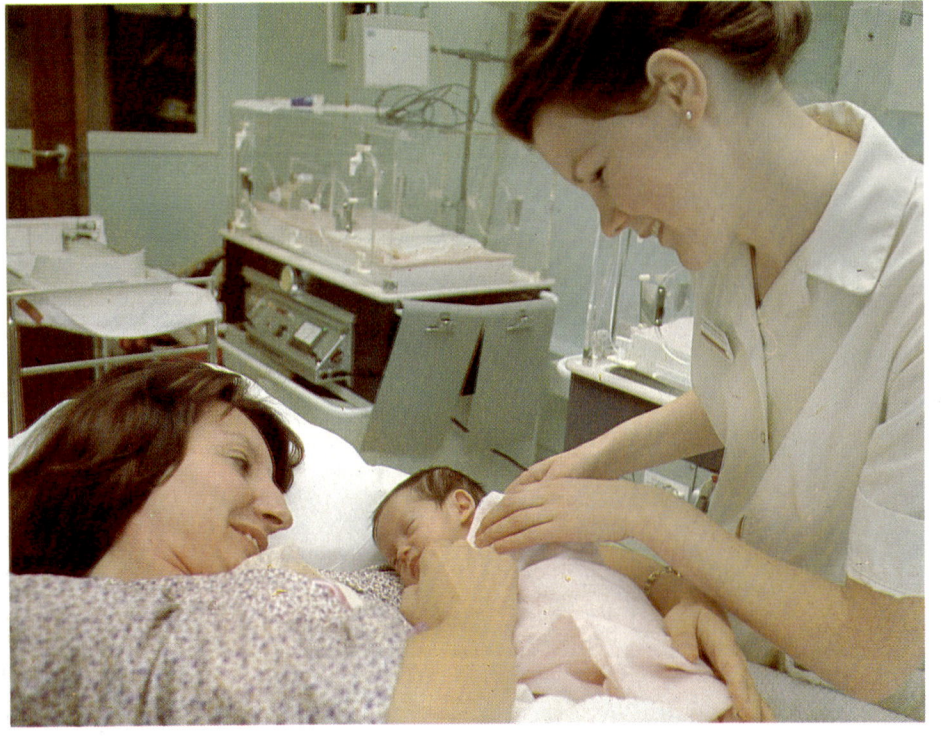

A nurse
shows a
mother her
new-born
baby.

Some babies are **premature** and need
special care after birth.
The doctor puts the baby into an
incubator like the one in our picture
to keep the baby warm and free from germs.
Nurses watch the baby carefully until
it has grown stronger and weighs more.

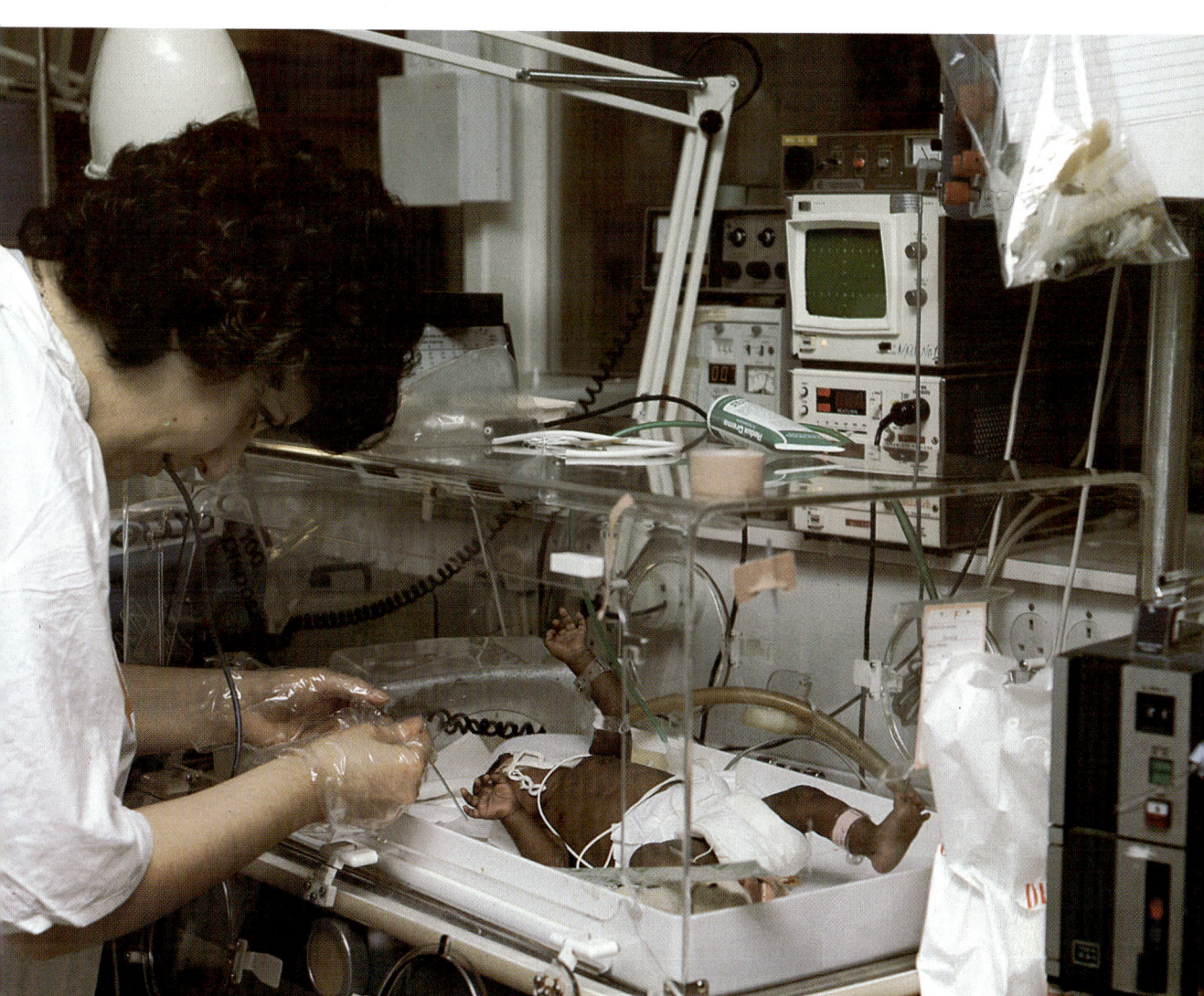

Nurses

Nurses take care of the patients in
the wards, and do much of the work in
the out-patients' clinics.

Nurses must understand how the
human body works and how to give the
patients their medicines.
They get patients ready for their
operations, and afterwards give the
patients any special care and any
necessary treatment.

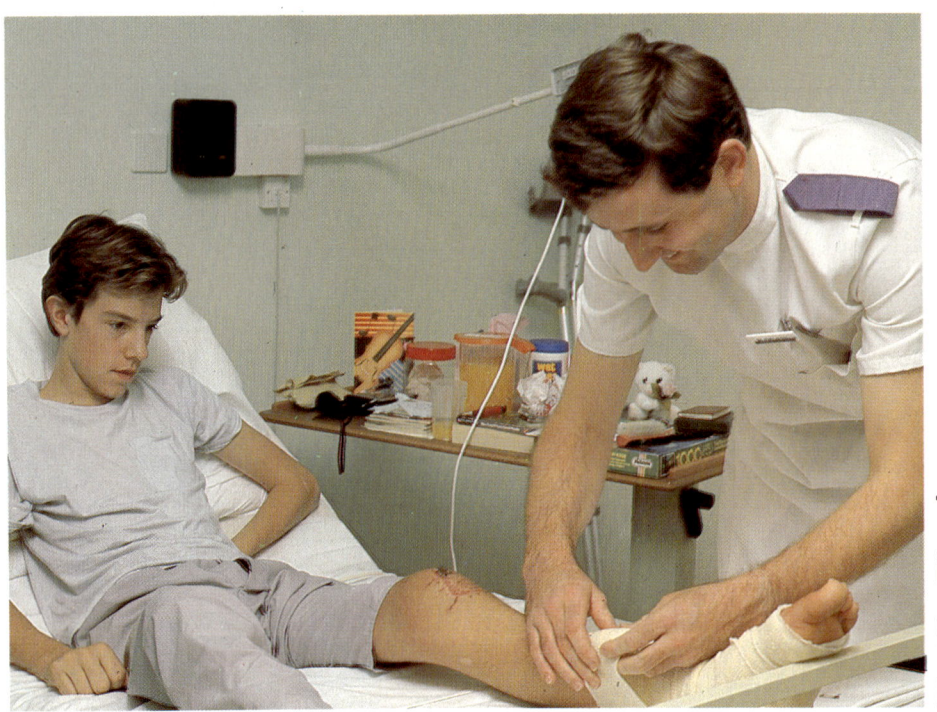

This male nurse
is caring for a
young
patient.

These student nurses work on the hospital wards as part of their training.

Nurses have to train for many years before they can be in charge of a ward.

Some nurses specialize in one branch of medicine. They may choose to become **midwives**, or to work with elderly people, or to work with children.
Some nurses who choose to work in the local area as health visitors visit people in their own homes.

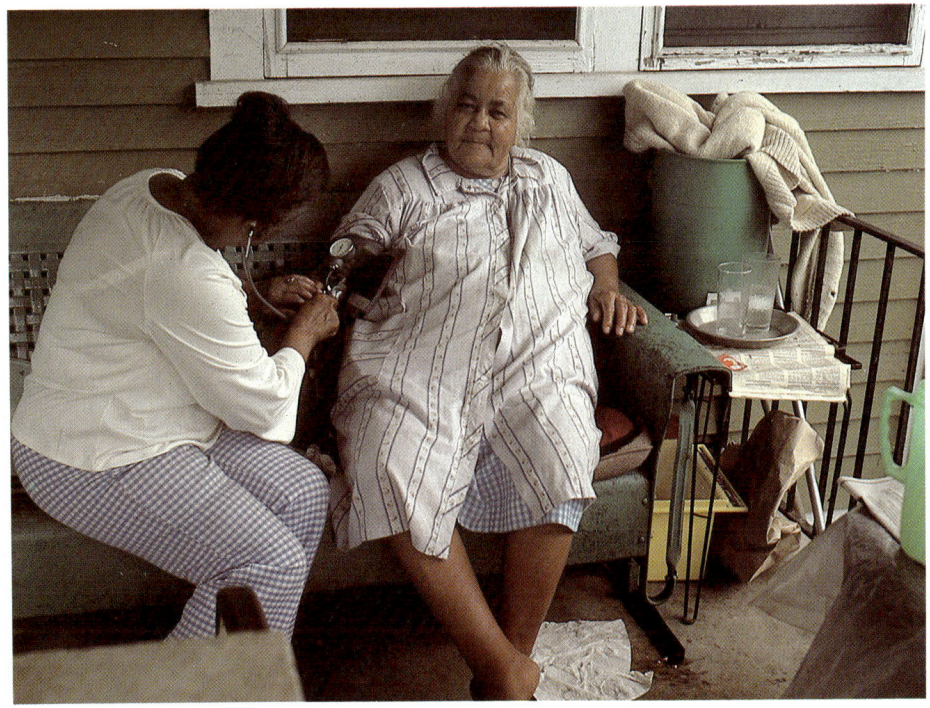

This health visitor is testing a patient's blood pressure.

23

Doctors

In the past women were not allowed to become doctors. Our picture shows Dr Elizabeth Blackwell, the first woman to become a doctor, in 1849.

Specialists and **surgeons** in a hospital train for many years to learn the best way to treat certain illnesses.

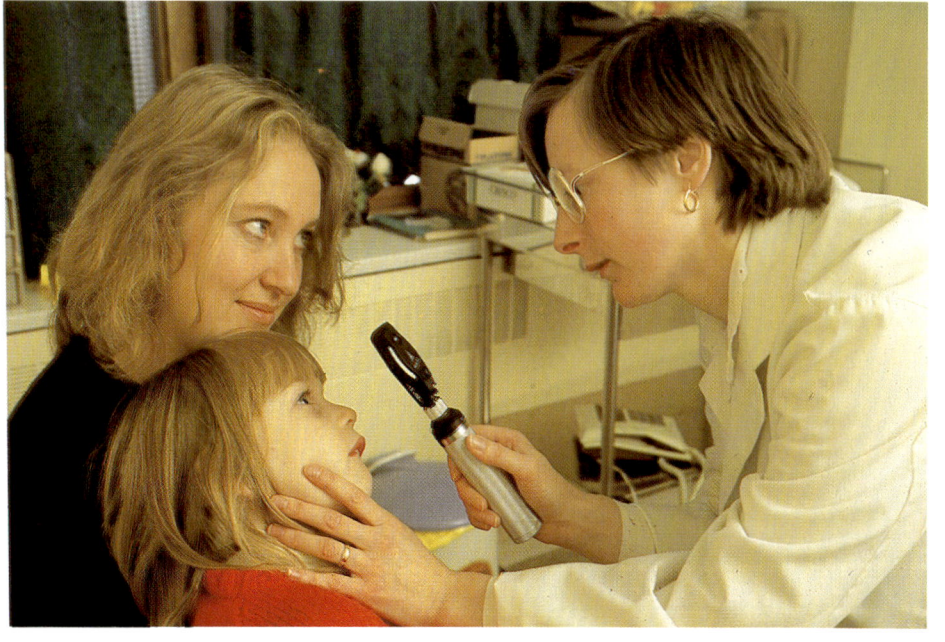

A specialist examining a child's eyes in an out-patient's clinic

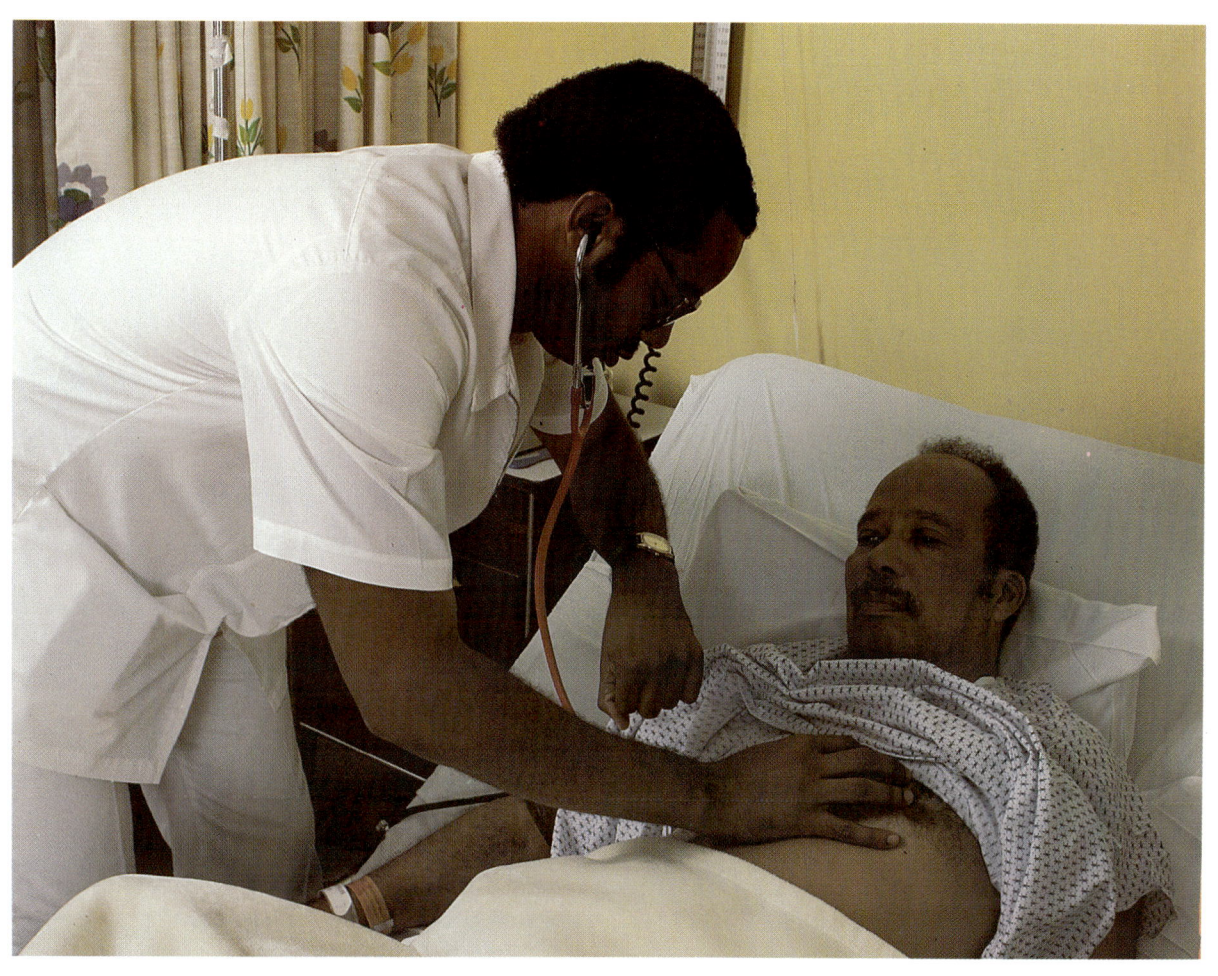

Specialists are helped by **junior doctors** who work with them as part of their training to learn how to treat different medical problems. Junior doctors often have to work very long hours in a hospital. They look after the patients when the specialist is busy, and handle any emergencies after an accident.

Looking into the body

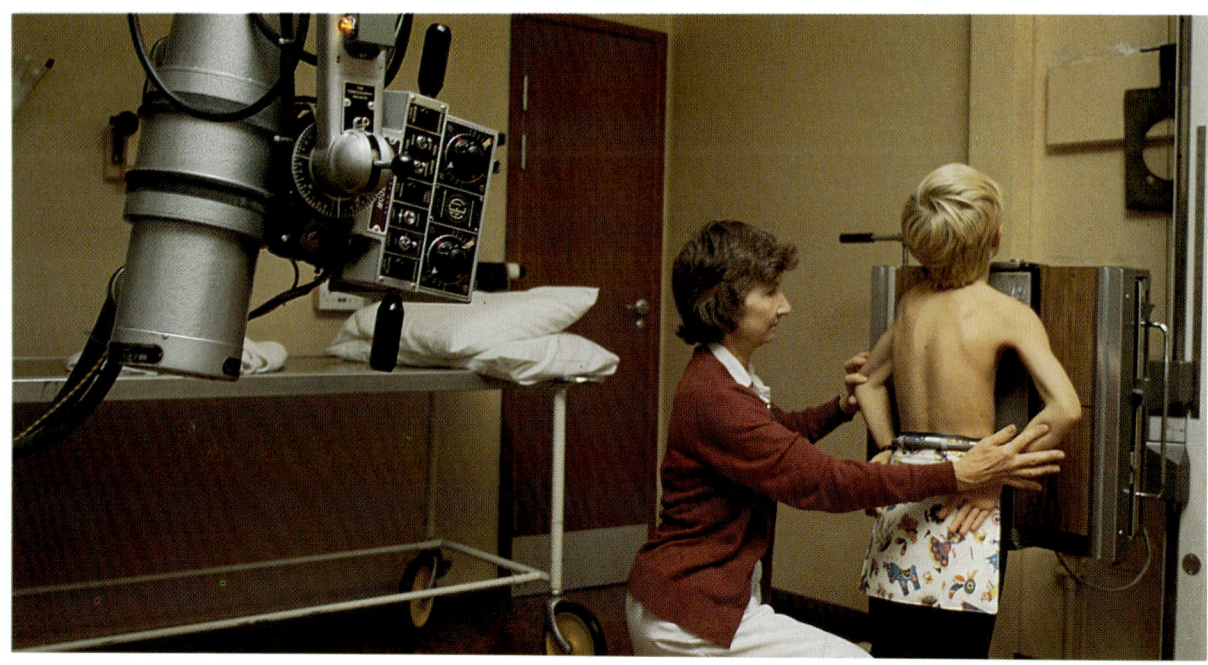

Sometimes a doctor needs to look inside a patient's body, to see if a bone is broken, or to look at other damaged parts of the body. The **radiographer** in the X-ray department can take a photograph of the injury.

An X-ray photograph of a broken leg bone

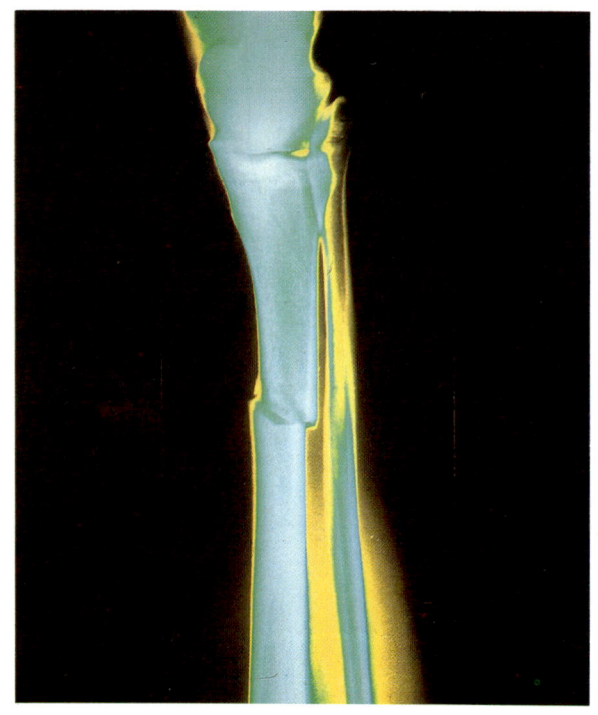

X-rays pass through the skin and
muscles of the patient and show up
the bones inside the body.
Doctors can also see X-rays as
pictures on a video screen.
Our picture shows a surgeon checking
an X-ray during an operation.
This will help the surgeon decide
what is wrong with the patient.

Ultrasound scanners can also help
the doctor look inside the body.
The scanners bounce **sound waves** off
different parts of the body.

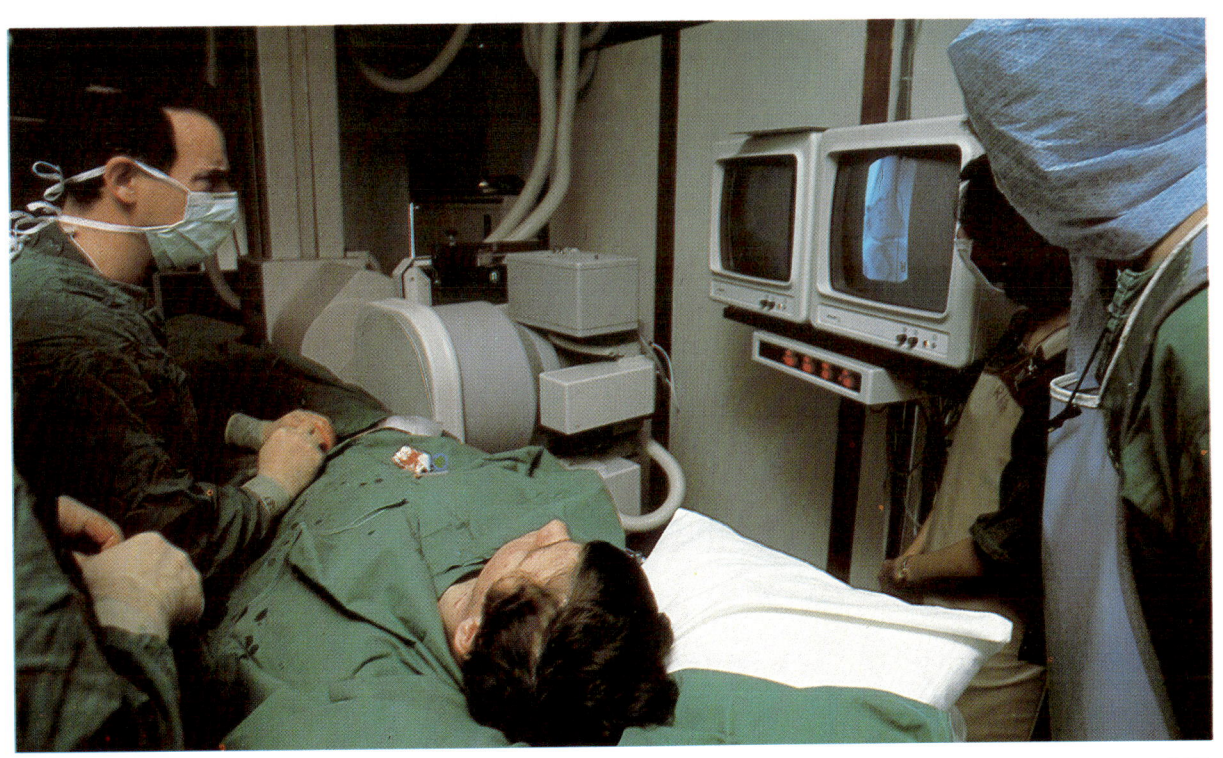

Preventing pain

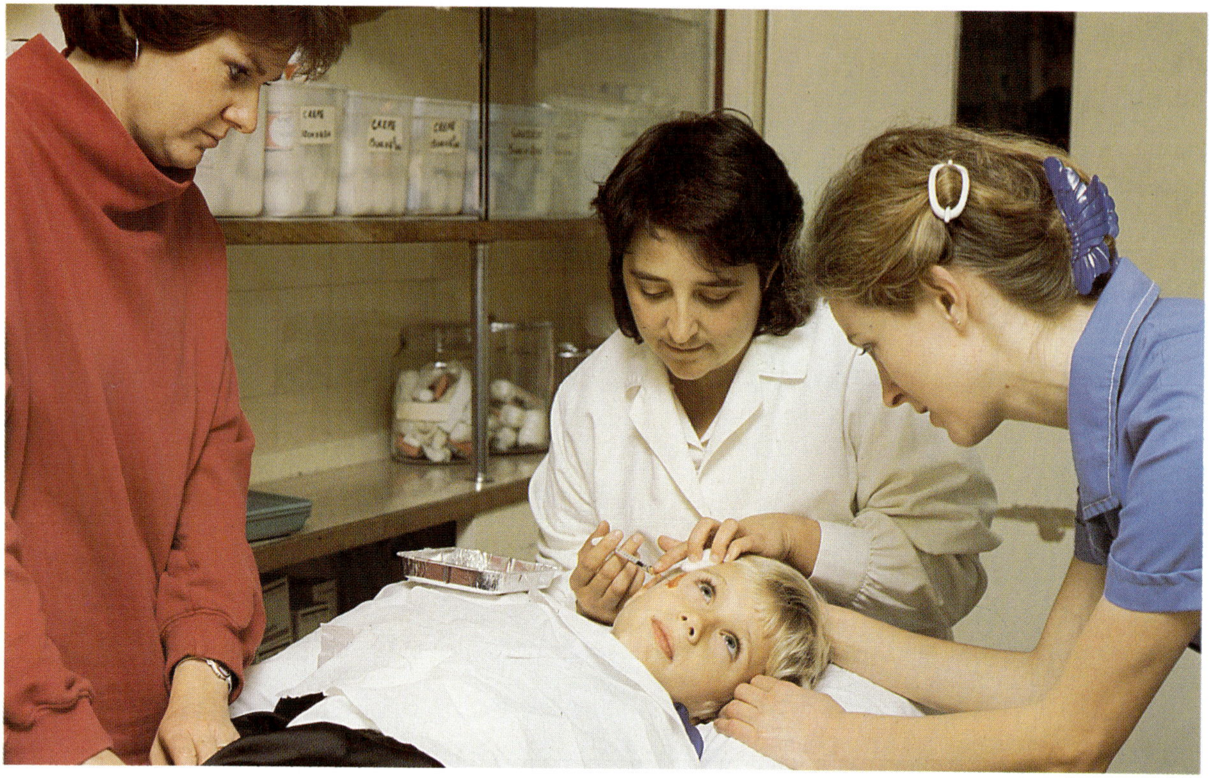

The boy in our picture has a bad head wound so the doctor is giving him an **injection** to take away the pain.

Patients are given an **anaesthetic** before they have an operation. A local anaesthetic numbs only part of the body, like this boy's head. A general anaesthetic sends the patient into a deep sleep.

The **anaesthetist** checks the patient during the operation and makes sure the patient has the right amount of anaesthetic.

A general anaesthetic causes problems for some patients, so some doctors use acupuncture instead. They stick needles into parts of the patient's body to block the nerves. The patient then feels no pain during an operation.

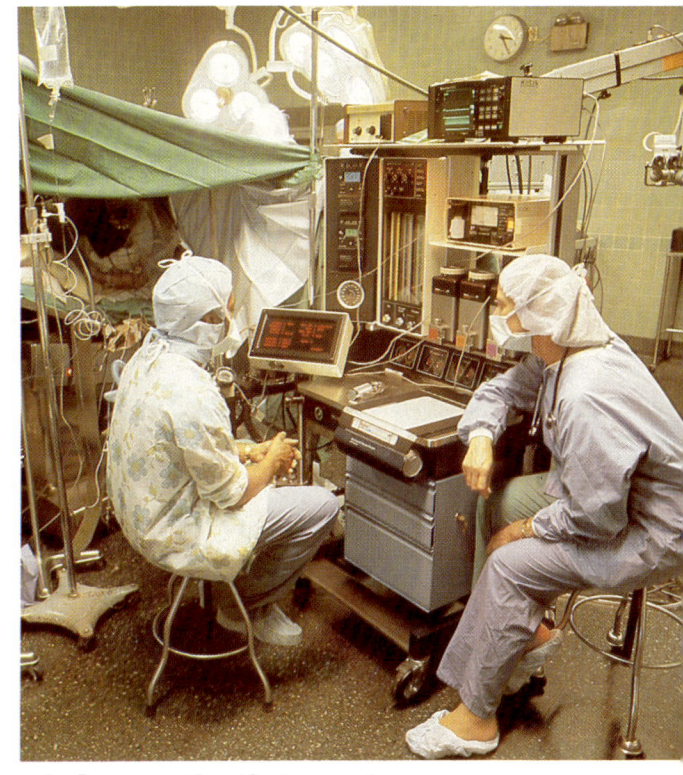

▲ **Anaesthetists using a computer to check the patient**

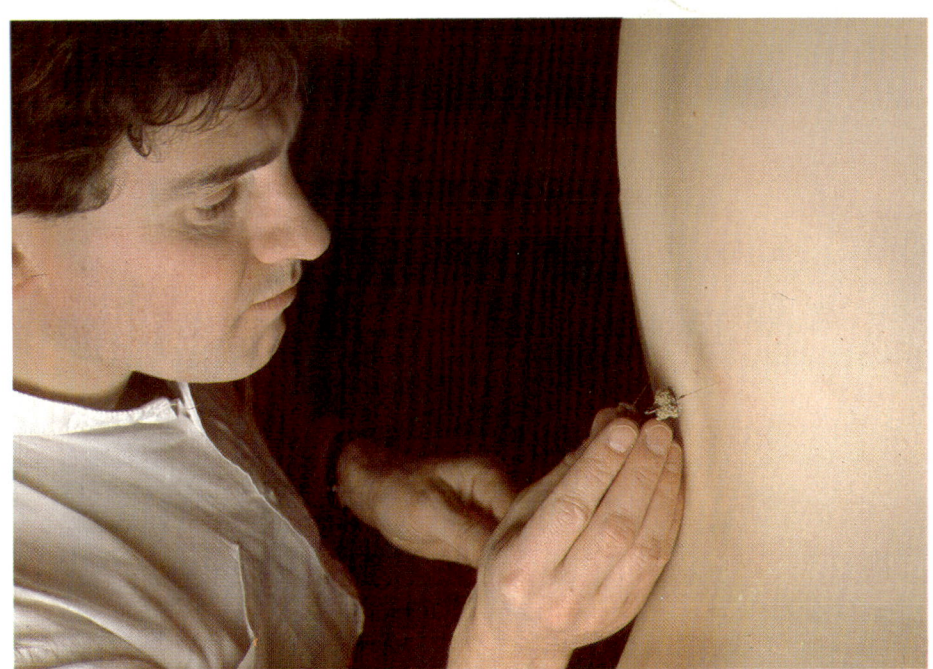

A patient having some acupuncture

The operating theatre

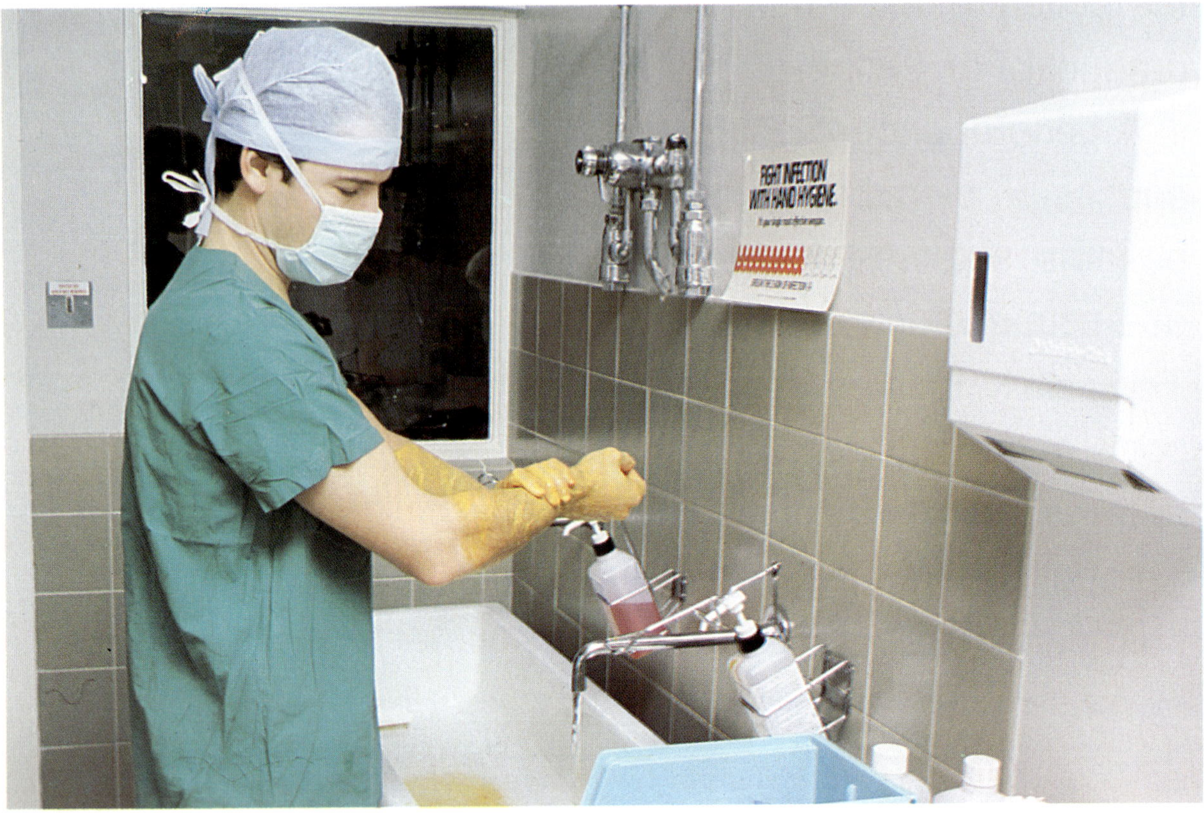

Before an operation, surgeons scrub their hands with **antiseptic**.
They put on gowns, gloves and masks to protect the patient from germs.

The **instruments** that the surgeon uses must be very clean as well.
After the surgeon has used them, the instruments are usually thrown away.

During the operation, the anaesthetist sits near the patient's head, and the nurses stand nearby, ready to pass the surgeon the necessary instruments.

Some simple operations only take a few minutes. Difficult heart operations often take many hours and need a team of surgeons.

Sometimes surgeons can't repair a damaged part of the body, and may replace it with a **transplant**, such as a new **cornea** in the eye.

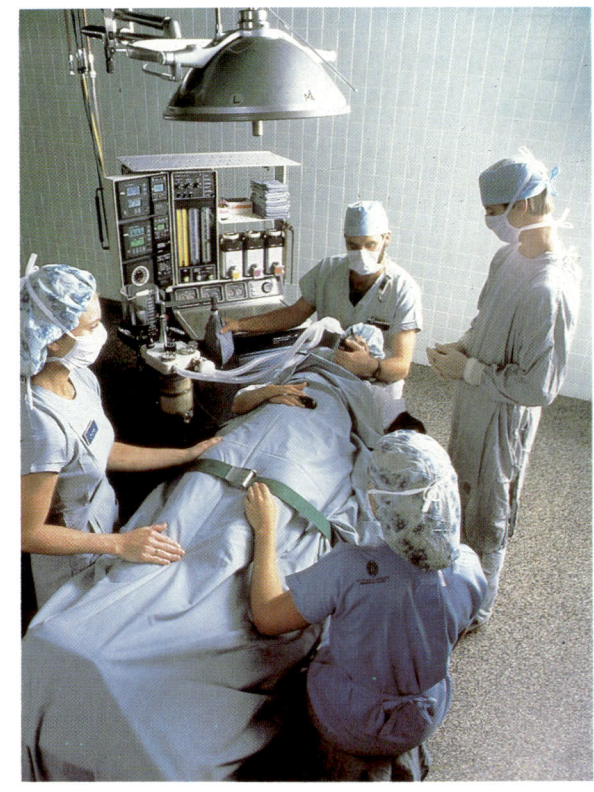

During the operation the patient lies on a special bed under a strong light.

After the transplant of a cornea this patient can now see well.

31

Getting moving

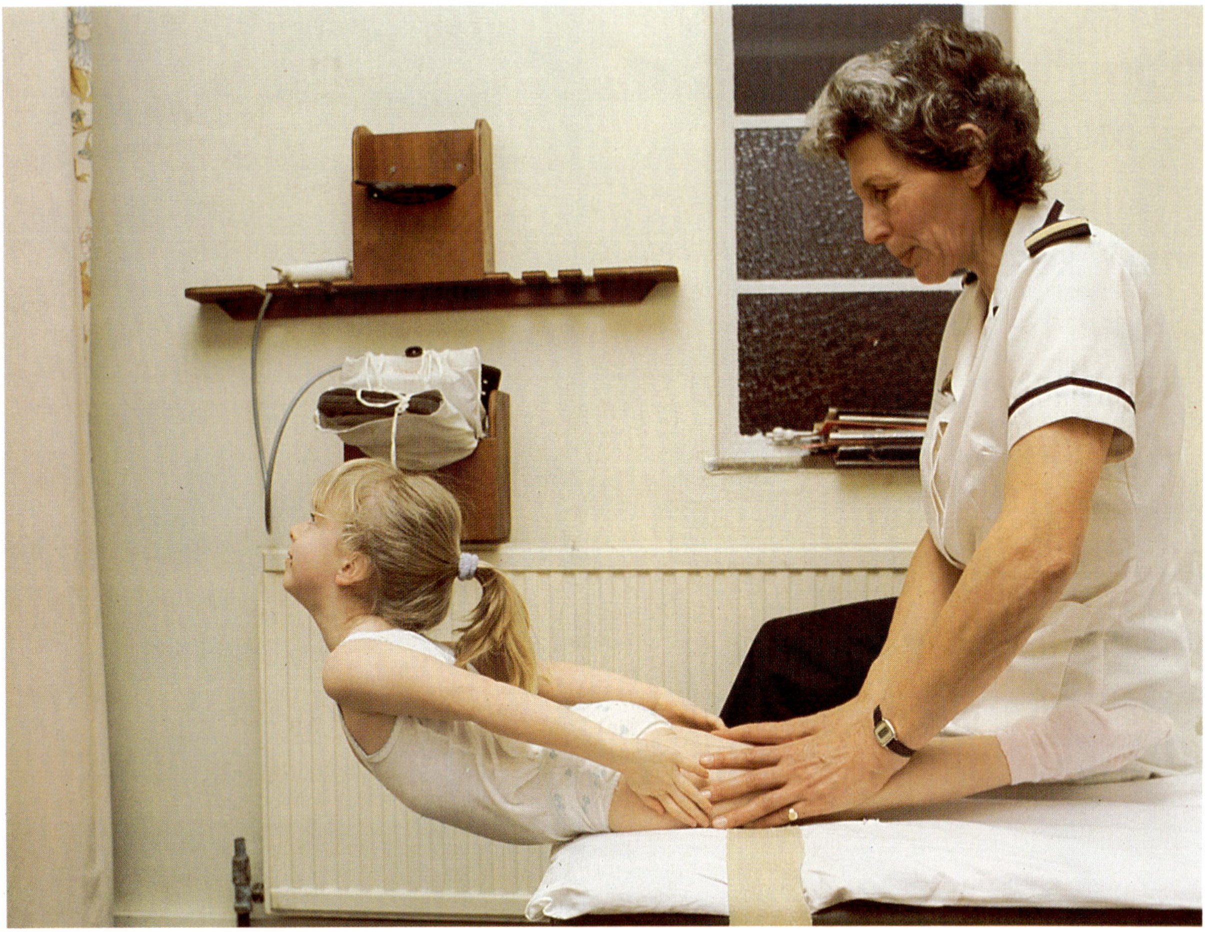

![Physiotherapy photograph]

After an operation, a patient's
muscles may be weak.
A physiotherapist works out a
programme of exercises to help the
patient strengthen weak muscles and
bones.

Exercise and physiotherapy in water
help many patients because the water
supports the weight of the body.
Physiotherapists also look after
people who have **physical handicaps**.

Patients in a swimming pool are helped to exercise.

Staff help physically handicapped patients enjoy sports.

Caring for the mind

Many people today suffer from **stress**.
They cannot relax from their busy
lives and may have a **nervous breakdown**.

Some people whose brains have been damaged, perhaps at birth, are mentally handicapped and may have trouble learning to do certain things. The boy in our picture is in a cookery class at a special school.

Other people suffer from mental illness and need treatment from a **psychiatrist** who will talk with them. The psychiatrist may use **analysis** to help them understand their illness.

Caring for the elderly

Hospitals often have special **geriatric wards** for elderly patients who become ill.

Elderly patients often take longer to recover from an illness and may need to stay in hospital for a long time.

In some parts of the world elderly people like this Chinese woman are cared for by their families so they may not need to go into hospital.

In other parts of the world, homes are too small for grandparents to live with their family, so they live in **sheltered housing** or in **retirement homes**. Nurses and other staff are always ready to help them.

Elderly women in a retirement home

Working in the laboratory

Laboratory workers help doctors find
the cause of different diseases.
They make tests for different germs.

There are two kinds of germs that cause disease.

Harmful **bacteria** can be destroyed by taking drugs called antibiotics.

Viruses are much smaller than bacteria.

Our photograph, taken under a **microscope**, shows a virus in someone's blood.

Scientists are trying to develop new **vaccines** to protect people from the viruses that cause disease.

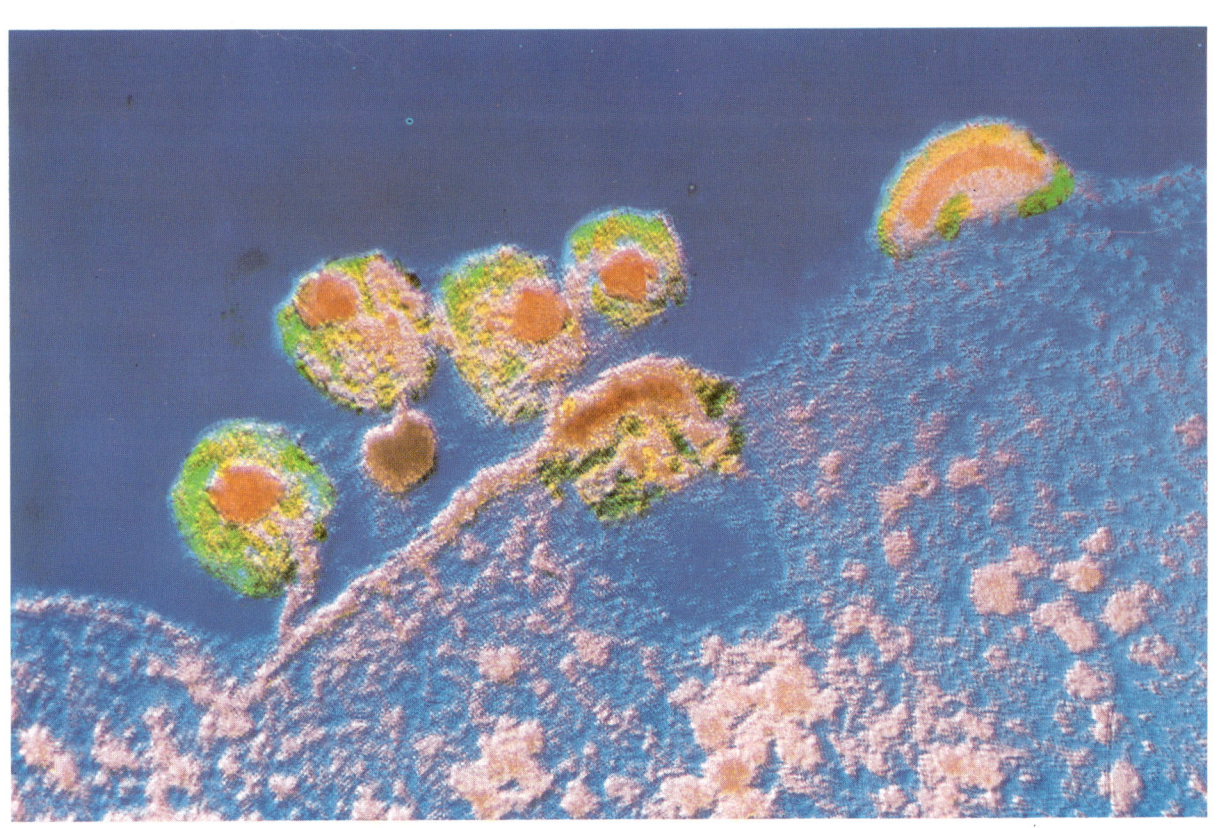

How are hospitals run?

Hospital administrators look after the day-to-day running of a hospital. The managers deal with any queries or complaints from patients, staff or public.

They pay the wages of the staff and make sure that there are enough medicines and equipment.

A hospital administrator works hard to make sure the hospital runs smoothly.

Hospitals have lots of drugs in their medical stores.

The hospital keeps the medical record
of every patient on file or on computer.
The records show what illnesses the
patient has had in the past, and what
treatments and medicines have been
given to the patient.

The hospital must also keep records
of all drugs and medical equipment.
It tells the local **health authority**
about different illnesses, births and
deaths.

Behind the scenes

There are many different jobs in hospitals. Telephonists on the hospital **switchboard** are busy day and night taking calls and messages. Electricians check that all the electrical equipment works well.

An electrician checks the wiring in a hospital.

The hospital wards and operating theatres must be kept spotlessly clean, and the patients must have clean bed linen.
The nurses change the beds regularly and send the sheets to the laundry.

In the hospital kitchens, the cooks make meals for the patients and staff. Some patients may need special kinds of food.
Dietitians make sure that each patient gets the right kind of food for their particular illness.

A changing world

Hospital administrators have to try
and plan ahead for the future needs
of a hospital.
Already the advances in medical
science allow premature babies a much
better chance of life.
People are now living longer, and
medical **researchers** are looking into
ways of improving the quality of life
for geriatric patients.

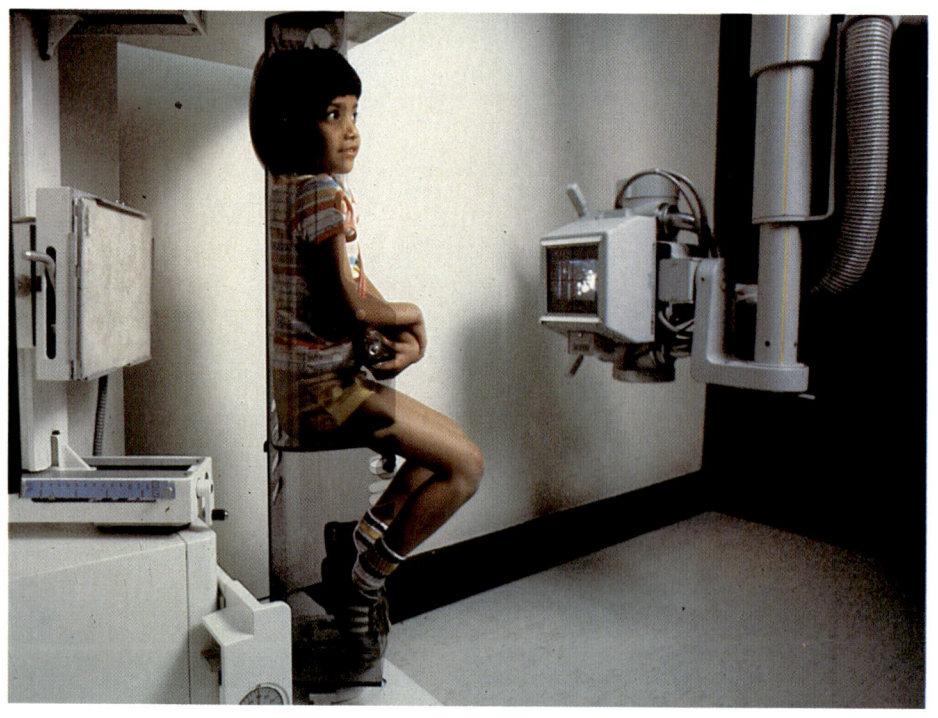

The X-ray
will show
if anything
is wrong
with this
child.

The scanner machine shows up the inside of the body on a screen.

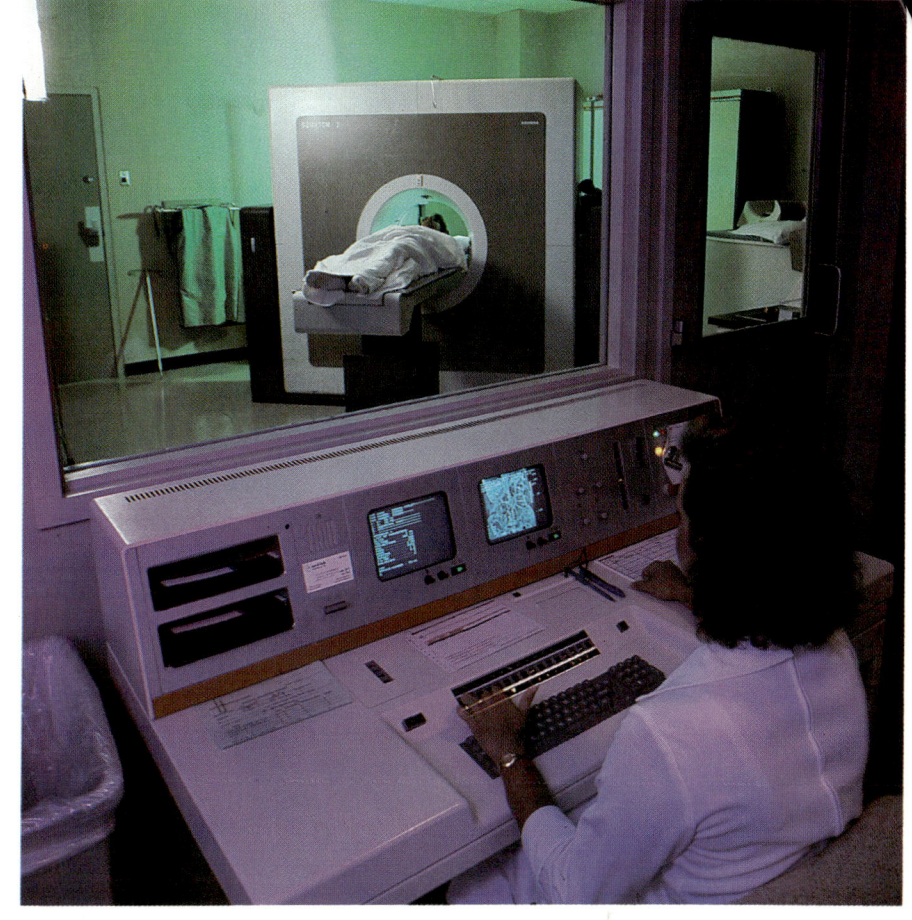

Medical research into how the human body works, and research into new drugs and treatments for the sick, will change the equipment that a hospital needs.

Our photograph shows a CAT scanner being used to help examine a patient. New inventions and new machines will change the way doctors and nurses take care of the sick in hospital.

Glossary

anaesthetic something used to stop a patient feeling pain

anaesthetist someone who specializes in working with anaesthetics

analysis treatment of a mental problem which involves the patient in thinking and talking about the problem

antiseptic something used to kill germs

bacteria tiny living things that can cause illness

blood pressure the amount of force needed to push blood around the body

clinic a place where a patient can see a doctor for a particular reason

cornea the transparent skin which covers the outer part of the eyeball

dietitian someone who knows what special foods patients with different illnesses need

disease an illness, usually caused by germs

emergency when a patient needs to see a doctor quickly

first aid treatment given to someone who has just had an accident

geriatric ward the ward in a hospital where elderly people are taken care of

germ a tiny living thing that can cause illness

health authority the organisation of an area that provides health care to the people living there

herbalist someone who uses herbs to cure sick people

infection an illness caused when germs get into a wound

injection a sharp instrument to put medicine into the body to cure illness or take away pain

instrument a tool used by the surgeon

junior doctor a newly trained doctor working in a hospital

laboratory a place where people try to find out about disease and new medicines

microscope an instrument that makes very tiny objects look a lot larger

midwives nurses who look after women when they give birth

nervous breakdown when people feel so mentally ill they cannot cope with everyday life

obstetrician a specialist who

cares for women when they are having babies

operation   the removal, replacement or repair of part of a patient's body

out-patient   somebody who goes to hospital for treatment, but does not stay there

paediatrician   a doctor who specialises in treating children's illnesses

paramedic   people with medical training who are not fully qualified as doctors

physical handicap   when unable to use one's body in a normal way

premature   a baby which is born before the normal pregnancy of nine months is ended

psychiatrist   a doctor who specializes in treating people with mental problems

radiographer   someone who takes X-ray pictures of a patient's body

receptionist   someone who greets visitors and gives them any information they need

researcher   someone who studies a particular problem

retirement home   a home where elderly people live together

sheltered housing   housing which allows elderly people to live on their own but which provides help in an emergency

sound waves   waves made by vibrations of the air which cause sound

specialist   a doctor who has made a special study of one part of the body

stress   when people feel exhausted from overwork

surgeon   a doctor who carries out operations

switchboard   where incoming telephone calls are put through to different people

transplant   the replacement of a damaged part of the body with a healthy part from another person

ultrasound   waves of sound which the human ear cannot hear which can be used to show the inside of a patient's body

vaccine   a substance used to prevent disease

virus   a tiny living thing that can cause illness

ward   a room in a hospital where patients stay

X-ray   an invisible ray which can be used to take pictures of inside the body from the outside

Index

Photographic credits

(t=top b=bottom l=left r=right)
cover: Science Photo Library; **title page:** Science Photo Library 4 Trevor Hill; 5 S. and R. Greenhill; 6t The Hutchison Library; 6b Vivien Fifield; 7 Mary Evans Picture Library; 8 Oxfam; 9t Novosti Press Agency; 9b S. and R. Greenhill; 12 Philip Steele; 13t, 13b S. and R. Greenhill; 14t ZEFA; 14b, 15 Science Photo Library; 16 ZEFA; 17t Trevor Hill; 17b The Hutchison Library; 18t Camille Jessel Photo Library; 18b The Hutchison Library; 19 Science Photo Library; 20 Biophoto Associates; 21 S. and R. Greenhill; 22 Trevor Hill; 23t St Bartholomew's Hospital; 23b S. and R. Greenhill; 24t BBC Hulton Picture Library; 24b Vision International; 25 Science Photo Library; 26t Trevor Hill; 26b, 27 Science Photo Library; 28 Trevor Hill; 29t Science Photo Library; 29b S. and R. Greenhill; 30 Trevor Hill; 31t Science Photo Library; 31b, 32 Trevor Hill; 33t Vision International; 33b, 34 The Hutchison Library; 35 S. and R. Greenhill; 36 The Hutchison Library; 37t S. and R. Greenhill; 37b Vision International; 38, 39 Science Photo Library; 40t Trevor Hill; 40b Science Photo Library; 41 Trevor Hill; 42t Science Photo Library; 42b 43 Trevor Hill; 44, 45 Science Photo Library